# Addie Clawson
## Appalachian Mail Carrier

By Julia Taylor Ebel
Art by Sherry Jensen

To Lorraine
another strong
lady!
Julia Taylor Ebel
April 25, 2006

**Parkway Publishers, Inc.**
Boone, North Carolina

*Available from:*
Parkway Publishers, Inc.
P. O. Box 3678
Boone, North Carolina 28607
Telephone/Facsimile: (828) 265-3993
*www.parkwaypublishers.com*

*Produced with support from the Central Piedmont Artists Hub Program and the North Carolina Arts Council and with a contribution from the National Postal Museum, Smithsonian Institution*

*Special thanks goes to those who graciously supported preparation of this book. Betty Lou Wells, Addie's daughter, shared many stories and photographs. Addie's other daughters, Sue Fairbrother and Rosalee Norris, contributed also. My husband Alan listened and chauffeured on missions to find facts and pictures of his Great Aunt Addie; my son John shared my interest in family stories. John R. Ebel provided calligraphy. Carole Weatherford and Don Greeson believed in me and shared artistic and professional knowledge that allowed me to move forward from writing into the pictorial processes. Brenda Beasley, archivist, Appalachian State University assisted in pictorial research. David Teague, Jamestown Public Library, answered many questions. Numerous Boone residents shared information, pictures, and leads: Pilar Moore, Sanna Gaffney, Johnny Graybeal, Daisy Adams, Earl Norris, Farthing Hayes, Floyd Benfield, Sandy Shook, Lucy Luther, Lucile Wallace, and others—many of whom remembered Miss Addie and offered fond recollections of her.—J.T.E.*

*Library of Congress Cataloging-in-Publication Data*

Ebel, Julia Taylor.
Addie Clawson : Appalachian mail carrier / by Julia Taylor Ebel ; art by Sherry Jensen.
p. cm.
Summary: Presents the story of Addie Clawson, the first woman mail Carrier in Boone, North Carolina, and her impact on the community. Includes bibliographical references.
1. Clawson, Addie. 2. Letter carriers—North Carolina—History—Juvenile Literature. [1. Clawson, Addie. 2. Letter carriers. 3. Sex role. 4. Women— Biography.] I. Jensen, Sherry, ill. II. Title.
HE 6499 .E24 2002
383'.49756843'092—dc 21
2002009496

*Editing, Layout and Book Design: Julie Shissler*
*Cover Design: Aaron Burleson*
*Cover Photo: Sue Fairbrother Collection*

*To the family, friends and neighbors*

*of Addie Hardin Clawson*

*and to all who deliver the mail*

**Addie Newton Hardin**
**Rutherwood, NC**
"Tho' the way be rugged she is determined to succeed."
From *The Rhododendron,* 1923, Appalachian Training School yearbook.
*University Archives, Appalachian State University*
*Photo: Rosalee Norris collection*

When Addie Clawson took the job of rural mail carrier, folks said it just wasn't right—a woman doing a man's job. Delivering babies and tending children was accepted as women's work in North Carolina's mountains in 1936. Addie Clawson knew she could deliver babies. She had even taught in one-room schoolhouses, but now she wanted to deliver the mail.

When Addie Clawson earned one of the top three scores on the Civil Service Examination, she got the job as rural mail carrier. Many of her neighbors doubted that she could handle the work. No matter what folks thought, Miss Addie was determined to be the best mail carrier in Watauga County.

**Rutherwood School, 1925**
Addie taught at several schools, including this one.
*Development of Public Education in Watauga County, North Carolina*, compiled by A Bicentennial Committee, Reka Shoemake, and others. Permission, Lucy Luther. *University Archives, Appalachian State University*

Addie Clawson with daughters Betty Lou and Mary Sue, and friend, Francis Shoemaker, 1938.
*Ella Mae Baird Collection*

Miss Addie was hired to work through spring and summer to deliver mail on Route 1, one of two rural mountain routes out of Boone, North Carolina. Postal officials thought that winter weather would make the route too rugged for small, lean Addie Clawson. They didn't know Miss Addie.

As soon as Miss Addie got the job, she bought a car. She purchased the car on Friday, learned to drive over the weekend, and was on the job on Monday driving her new Chevrolet.

**US Highway 421 near Boone.**
Addie's mail route, initially 24 miles, was extended to 53 miles after the Laxon post office closed in 1952. No more than 12 miles were paved.
*North Carolina Office of Archives and History, Raleigh, North Carolina*

Miss Addie drove up the mountain road to Boone and picked up the mail at the post office. She drove down the road again to deliver the mail along the way—around Bamboo Road and Brown's Chapel Road, out Pine Run Road and deep into the hills.

In those days, the only paved road was the narrow, winding highway that went up to Boone and down to Deep Gap. Dirt and gravel roads wove around the hills and into hollows. Some of those roads were too rough for a car, so Addie's husband, Bland, met her along the route with a horse. Her horse could take her where her car could not go. Bland traded the horse for the car and later met Addie to swap again.

**U.S. Post Office, Boone, North Carolina.**

*L.C. LeCompte Collection, University of North Carolina at Asheville, Ramsey Library Special Collections.*

*Permission, Lake County, IL, Discovery Museum, Curt Teich Postcard Archives*

Miss Addie dressed in jodhpurs, English riding pants, so she could climb on her horse to ride the roughest paths. Once she rode a mule. Folks saw her coming and exclaimed, "There's Miss Addie on a mule!" She greeted them with her ready smile and a friendly word.

In the 1930s, women just didn't wear pants. Some ladies were appalled to see Miss Addie wearing jodhpurs. When they complained to the pastor, he said, "I think it'd pay me to mind my own business."

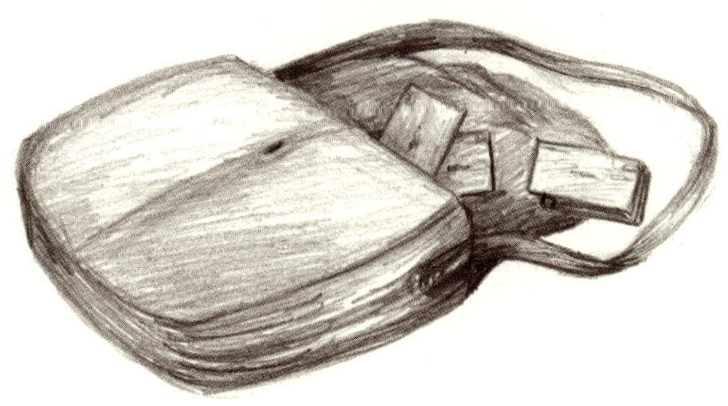

**Downtown Boone**

Deep snow near the Post Office soon after Addie began delivering mail.

*Historic Boone Archives*

Spring surprised everyone with a blizzard. Snow piled deeply and drifted to even greater depths. Roads were closed for three weeks, but Miss Addie pressed on. Snow, sleet, or blizzard could not delay her for long. Miss Addie soon delivered the mail—and she kept her job.

Still, Miss Addie's car had trouble on the rocky roads and stream crossings. She traded for a Model A Ford because it was built with a body higher off the ground.

When time came for the postmaster to inspect Miss Addie's rural route, she suggested, "We'd better take my car, Mr. Hartzog." The postmaster wasn't interested in giving up his fine car to ride in Miss Addie's Model A Ford. Sure enough, the postmaster's car couldn't ford the New River at Pine Run Road. The engine drowned. Miss Addie waded across the river and walked to the nearest farm to get the farmer and his horse to pull Mr. Hartzog's car out of the river.

Miss Addie's Model A served her well until 1950, when she decided that a Jeep would travel better on the rugged roads. So Addie sent her son-in-law to Michigan to buy an Army Jeep. Her Jeep was the first one in the area. She later replaced the canvas-covered Army Jeep with a Jeep station wagon that could keep out rain and cold.

Addie mailed the front envelope home from the national postal convention in 1946.
The cancellation mark notes the fiftieth anniversary of rural mail delivery.
*Nate Grubb, Photographer.*
*Envelopes: University Archives, Appalachian State University, and Betty Lou Wells Collection*

Miss Addie delivered more than mail and messages. She sometimes picked up groceries or medicine in town for folks along her route who didn't own cars. Some children thought she even delivered baby brothers and sisters.

Miss Addie and her daughter, Betty Lou, often helped neighbors mail Christmas cards. Miss Addie and Betty Lou would take the cards and stamp money to town, buy the stamps, stick them on the envelopes, and then put the cards in the mail.

The first Christmas stamps were issued in 1962.
*Permission, National Postal Museum, Smithsonian Institution*

At Christmas, many mountain folks ordered their gifts from the Montgomery Ward and Sears, Roebuck & Company catalogs. Miss Addie delivered the mail every Christmas Eve and then went home in the afternoon to eat supper with her family. Late on Christmas Eve, though, she made one more delivery of the packages that had arrived at the Boone Post Office during the day. Addie Clawson wasn't going to leave the children on her route waiting for their gifts on Christmas morning!

Folks learned they could count on Miss Addie to deliver the mail. To thank her, they sometimes left a little something at the mailbox—apples, vegetables, or cookies.

One day when Miss Addie reached for her lunch, it wasn't there. She had forgotten to put it in the car. At the very next house, Callie Walls stood at the mailbox and waited for Miss Addie.

"I've seen you go by with just a bag lunch and thought you might like a hot meal," Callie said, holding out a tray of warm food.

Children, including her grandson, Johnny Simmons, met Miss Addie on her route.
*Betty Lou Wells Collection. Permission, The Watauga Democrat*

Children also met Miss Addie at the mailboxes. She gave them advertising fliers so they'd have their own mail.

One day little Tommy Critcher asked, "Have you got any mail for me?" Miss Addie handed him a flier. He looked at it and then back at Miss Addie. "I want some real mail," he said with a stomp of his foot.

That night Miss Addie asked her daughters to write letters to Tommy so he'd get some real mail.

*Dear Tommy*

*Mama said she saw your new puppy yesterday. What did you name him? I remember when my dog was a puppy. We had such fun running and romping in the field.*

"Neither snow, nor rain, nor heat, nor gloom of night stays these couriers from the swift completion of their appointed rounds."
*Inscribed at the main New York City Post Office, adapted from Herodotus*

Miss Addie delivering mail after the blizzard in March of 1960.
*Betty Lou Wells Collection. Permission, The Watauga Democrat*

Miss Addie delivered mail in rain and snow. Folks sometimes waited for her to come through to break up a new snow before they ventured out.

Miss Addie traveled with her shovel. In winter she used it to clear snowdrifts. After rains she used it to dig out of the mud.

One winter, ice blocks stopped Miss Addie's car in a stream crossing. She used the shovel and poles handed to her from the bank to push away the ice—but not before the seat of her car got wet from the rising water.

*Betty Lou Wells Collection*

Miss Addie's equipment also included an ax. Her ax was handy when wind and storms left trees across the road.

One time Miss Addie found a big tree fallen across Wilson Ridge Road. The only person nearby was tiny Mrs. Cook, but the two of them rolled up their sleeves, gripped the handles of a cross-cut saw, and went to work. Together they cleared the road.

The flood of 1940 washed out roads and bridges along Addie's route and throughout the region.
*The Jefferson Post. Permission, Lucile Wallace*

Shovel, ax, and borrowed tools weren't enough to get Miss Addie through in 1940. Floods washed out seven bridges on her route, including the New River bridge between her home in Rutherwood and the Boone Post Office. No one could go up or down the mountain road.

The flood even washed out the tracks for the narrow-gauge train that ran through the mountains. Tweetsie, as folks call the train, had carried not only passengers but bags of mail between Boone and Johnson City, Tennessee.

**Tweetsie**, the East Tennessee and Western North Carolina/Linville River train at the Boone station, 1930s.
*Johnny Graybeal, East Tennessee and Western North Carolina Railroad Historical Society; Jim Dowdy Collection*

**Addie after the blizzard of 1960**
*Betty Lou Wells Collection*

Only once more did weather ground Miss Addie. In 1960 six weeks of snowstorms piled drifts as high as eighteen feet. Watauga, Ashe, and Avery counties were declared disaster areas. Helicopters dropped emergency deliveries of food, clothing, and messages. In spite of the snow, Miss Addie was soon out with her shovel. She had to reach way down to the mailboxes, but she delivered the mail.

For thirty years folks down the hill from Boone knew their mail was coming. Addie Clawson proved to be a woman fit for a "man's job."

**Addie delivers the mail, March 1960**
*Betty Lou Wells Collection*

## *Sources*


Chumblee, Wayne. "Addie Shares Tales of Delivering Mail on Horseback, Living During the Depression," Appalachian Oral History Project. *The Watauga Democrat*, February 3, 1973.

Ellis, Ruby. "She Still Brings the Mail Through." *The Watauga Democrat*, 1957 (no date).

Ellis, Ruby. "Woman to Make Last Appointed Round." *The Watauga Democrat*, December 30, 1965.

Greene, Ivery C. *A Disastrous Flood: A True and Fascinating Story.* Deep Gap, NC, 1941.

Norris, Rosalee. "Addie Newton Hardin Clawson." *The Heritage of Watauga County, North Carolina,* Vol. II. Curtis Smalling, Editor. Southern Appalachian Historical Association. Winston-Salem, NC: Hunter Publishing Co., 1987.

Nunnelee, Nixie. "Mrs. Addie Clawson." *Forever Alive: Mountain People, Mountain Land.* Appalachian State University, 1978.

Rivers, Rachel. "Mrs. Addie Clawson Retires after 30 Years of Service." *The Watauga Democrat*, January 1966.

Shoemake, Reka W., and others. *Development of Public Education in Watauga County, North Carolina.* Compiled by A Bicentennial Committee, 1976.

**Miss Addie retires after 30 years of service**
*Betty Lou Wells Collection. Permission, The Watauga Democrat*